The Isinglass River

Poems by

Carol Leavitt Altieri

Goose River Press
Waldoboro, Maine

Library of Congress Card Number: 2003104957

ISBN: 1-930648-53-7

First Printing, 2003

Cover photo by Connie DelVisco.

Published by
Goose River Press
3400 Friendship Road
Waldoboro ME 04572
dbenner@prexar.com
www.gooseriverpress.com

Acknowledgements

The following poems have appeared in the journals and anthologies to which grateful acknowledgement is made. My special thanks to the editors of the following:

Anthology of New England Writers 1997 "On the Beach at Crest Haven, Kittery, Maine"
Re: Vision 1994"Gondola Lifts Us" and "In Beijing, There Are No Dawn Redwoods"
Connecticut Environmental Journal "Acorn Whistle for Bethany Wanderers" 1995
Connecticut Review 1998 "Ambushed"
Connecticut River Review 1995 "In Beijing, ...; "Song for the Wilderness Champion"
Eclectic Rainbows "Lake District's Dry Stone Walls" 1996
Family Earth 1996 "Peterson's Poems" 1996
Southern CT. State University Folio: 1994 "In Beijing,...,"
Gathering Swallows 1997 "Celebrating Spring"
Moose Bound Press: "From Riez to Moustiers ; "Plovers, Dowitchers...," "Song for the Wilderness Champion" 1996; 1997
The Journal of Graduate Liberal Studies, Spring 1998: "Peggy's Cove" and "Hiking Killington"
RE: Vision 1994 "Gondola Lifts Us in New Zealand"
Shells: 1996 "Exxon Valdez"
The Connecticut Writer 1996 " Your Symbol is a Garden"
The Lowell Pearl 1996 "The Heavens Scourge Us Too"
Touch the Earth 1995 "An Acorn Whistle for Bethany Wanderers"
Tributaries, A Journal of Nature Writing, Owl Walk Press, 1998: "The Commander and the Spotted Owls" and "On the Beach at Crest Haven, Kittery, Maine"
Verseweavers, The Oregon State Poetry Association Anthology of Prize-winning Poems 1999 "In Oswego at SUNY Seeking the Spirit of William Butler Yeats"
Whisper: 1996 "Shelling the "Pearl of the Adriatic"
Writer's Unlimited 1997 "Luck"

Table of Contents

Table of Contents

Special Thanks

Grateful acknowledgement is made to the editors of the following journals in which poems have appeared, some in slightly rewritten versions:

Anthology of New England Writers, Connecticut Environmental Journal, Connecticut Review, Connecticut River Review, Eclectic Rainbows, Family Earth, Shells, Gathering Swallows, Folio, Monadnock, Moose Bound Press, Massachusetts Journal of Graduate Liberal Studies, Oregon Poetry Journal, Poetry Forum, The Connecticut Writer, The Lowell Pearl Touch the Earth, Tributaries, Verse Weavers, The Oregon State Poetry Anthology of Prize-winning Poems, A Journal of Nature Writing, Vision Whisper, Writer's Unlimited among others.

I am indebted to Dr. Sue Holloway who is linked to me by mind, heart and soul with the touchstone of nature, on this declining planet. You encouraged and urged me on, strongly critiqued my poems, appreciated my efforts, and joined in creative excitement.

I am especially aware of the debt to my friends and fellow poets: Claire Zoghb, Sally Belenardo, Jane Kellogg, Elizabeth Possidente and Jean Vulté who have stimulated me in many ways over the last four years. You have been unfailingly helpful. Thank you for your faith in me.

My deepest thanks to Connie DelVisco, retired art teacher in Orange, Connecticut, for artistic contributions. My soul sister for forty years, I am very grateful to you for artwork and creative imagery for two Mexican poems.

Special thanks to Dr. Vivian Shipley for continual encouragement and critiques, which greatly refined, layered, and deepened my poems. Also, you stimulated me to take "imaginative leaps," which helped my poetry grow with passion, complexity, and emotional energy.

Moreover, I am aware of my debt to Tony Connor who encouraged me to write about what I thought was an insignificant life. My special gratitude for your artistic gifts of thoroughness and originality that will be forever planted in my writings. You provided invaluable advice and support as the poetry took shape—very real points of illumination.

Special gratitude to Edwina Trentham for your knowledge and good examples and for pushing me harder toward more ecological and poetic force.

In addition, Frank, Frank Scot, Alicia and Michael who affirmed and critiqued, inspiring me to greater power with your accomplishments, interests, and artistry, who have supported me emotionally all the years, and who have helped the book reach fruition.

May I suggest: Realize your own contributions and believe in the marvelous nature of Creation and the role humans must play as its stewards.

DEDICATED TO:

Henry Ferris—

mentor, director of Menunkatuck Audubon Society,
extraordinary artist, natuarlist, writer,
ethical and thoughtful community man.

In *The Isinglass River,* Carol Altieri urges us to believe *in the marvelous nature of Creation and the role Humans must play as its stewards.* These poems are deeply felt prayers for the world, meditations presented by an emotionally complex mind. Altieri is a priest giving a communion wafer, offering salvation to a world that is deeply troubled. She sees things *not alone, / but connected and linked/ to all other congregations.* Vibrant with life, her poems keep us alert by their honest and serious questioning of the destruction of wildlife and men. Yet, as she kneels down to plant a butterfly bush, or touches green frogs with her grandson, Altieri's voice is filled with hope, with spring. Tying disparate experience together with her overarching vision, Altieri takes us to Blanco Turbi where turtles are threatened by poachers and to Phillip's Island, Australia, to watch Fairy penguins parade. Other poems give witness to man's destruction of sea otters by Valdez oil nets and to sequoias and redwoods being scavenged for chip mills that grind them for pulp. Altieri persuades us to travel where the poems take us, even if that involves learning to hear a boy weeping in Zaire, or to see faces in Dubrovnik as they are bombarded by Serbian tanks. Altieri knows we must listen for the individual cry in the din. The poems echo, reverberate with meaning and give us new perceptions, insights into the world we inhabit, helping us to understand that even as the ovenbird builds a nest shaped like a brick store, a striped snake swallows a toad. Reading these poems, I was taken back to a place I was introduced to by Ovid and Euripides, a place where humans are caught by powers that cannot be controlled. Altieri faces the world, but offers us the consolation of an intelligent human spirit who struggles with the blackness and is not broken. Showing us what one person can do by paying tribute to Jacques-Yves Cousteau, Altieri's poems prompt us to ban nuclear sites in order to protect spawning rites for salmon, and inpire *us to save all life/for future humans to know-.* Her poems show us that we must not refuse to look away from the world, from its terror or from its ravishing beauty. They teach our hearts to persevere.

—*May 23, 2003*
Vivian Shipley
Editor of Connecticut Review

The Isinglass River

Together in Childhood

We have walked thigh-high in wildflowers. The natural world....holds
us close and lets us revel in the intimacy of all that is real.
—Terry Tempest Williams, *Refuge*

In deep woods, pink lady slippers prance.
I pull home my little
sister curled up in a red dog cart
under an egg yolk sun.

Oven birds flutter north
in early spring. A pair sculpt a nest
shaped like a brick oven to hatch
speckled eggs lisping out
the "Teacher, Teacher" song.

Down on the pond, marsh marigolds
float like gnome's faces
and spring peepers murmur
under skirts; I see a striped
snake devour a toad.

The Holstein suckles her calf
in the orchard and my sister
turns cartwheels where
pear trees blossom
and cherries ripen.

Later, after twilight, I trudge home
from haying, bone weary
and sweating on a moon-scented
evening sparkled by flickering
lightening bugs. I spot
the tiny brown bat clinging tightly
to its mother.

1

Filling Our Buckets

Instead, my father, two sisters
and I tapped the sap of maple
trees, filling buckets,
sliding them out on sleigh,
boiling forty gallons of sap
for one sweet one.

Priming well water
with long-handled pump
and drawing water with dipper,
we reveled in alchemy
making more from less.

Curtains sewn from feed sacks,
hand-down clothes created
family heirlooms.
Our voices subdued
from so much labor....
From cornmeal,
Indian pudding, eggs gathered
from Rhode Island Reds.

I climbed sheer granite
faces of White Mountains,
strengthened my muscles
and kept the chlorophyll
flowing in my veins.

Poem Written from Flag Hill, 1942-1954

Chores carved our lives,
like the Flume Gorge
of Old Man of the Mountains.
My family held one hundred fifty acres
there in Flag Hill, New Hampshire.

Our Holsteins and Guernseys
galumphed to barn; corralled
into stanchions.
My dad pitched hay into troughs
shaking down more from the rafters,
molding teat cups to pink udders
as milking machine clock ticked
throbbing out the golden elixir.

Our marrow made
of the Great Depression
and muscles tightened by World War II.

Seven days times sixteen—
watered, grained, shoveled,
hayed, plowed, planted, winnowed,
and harvested.

I rose with a burst of roosters
crowing and soon the chickens cackled
when I fetched their eggs.

Near the sugar maples, I sloshed
through streams and creeks,
leading cows to pasture. Parsing out time,
they cowered in woodlands.
When their milk dried, what could our
poor creatures do
about "Live Free or Die"?

The Hurricane

The day the hurricane
rampaged the neighborhood
leaving battle scars,
I witnessed winds ripping
ancient oaks to jackstraws;
beech, and old maples overthrown.

Whirlwinds subverted trailers,
maimed privet hedges
and raided evergreen woods.
Much later, leaving memory
craters; stumbling over
limbs and moss cobblestones,
I hear a dripping faucet
and woodpeckers
pock-marking pines.

Visitors arrive with
out-of-state license plates
carting cornucopias. They
race backhoes and spin chain
saws; clear wrenched debris,
hammer down shingles,
while from back yards
mourning doves coo.

Halloween

I walked home alone, taking
the five-mile short-cut
over the logging road
after the party. A yellow
birch tree, leaves torn away
by strong winds, thrown across
the road. Two farmers' sons
buried under dead leaves sprang
out. Dry lightning split a maple
tree. I kicked, screamed, and
howled in an all-out attack.

Writhing in combat, I rolled
out on top. Sumac tangled my
ankles. Thorns and nettles
tore my legs like hands ripping
my jeans as I flew home—
a panther in the darkness.

The knob rattled on the hollow door.
I crept up the stairs and
crawled under the feather
blanket, trying to smother myself
to sleep as the night sank into
coiled oblivion.

Trailing Arbutus (Mayflower)

My dad brings a bouquet to me,
most treasured, newly-sprouted mayflowers.
In April, sweet fragrance from forest edge,
like rarity of bloodroot or yellow ladyslippers.

Trailing leathery leaves and woody stems
peeking and pushing from spring
earth, hiding under heart-shaped leaves.
The earliest, tinged pink, spread their petals,
perfumed and spry, ushering in warmth
to lead way for lilacs, columbines,
trilliums, Quaker-ladies, and Solomon's seals.
All join the woodland show,
bowing like courtiers before a queen,
as my dad plays his harmonica
and I hear rills and ripples
of our Isinglass River.

Breathe deeply and inhale the fragrance
symbolizing deep, unspoken love.
In shady places of clumps and patches,
flowers commingle with earth
scent and apple blossom essence.
In heaven now, my dad clutches
a bouquet of mayflowers. Some wildflowers linger
in pockets of mind;
I cultivate their sanctuaries for retreat.

Luck

From the earliest time, you
didn't cushion me—instead
you placed me in the bureau
drawer to sleep and left me
tossing and cramped until I
grew older and ran away
so many times I don't remember.
I told rescuers who found me,
"I'm hitch-hiking to Canada."

You often talked to yourself
gesticulating wildly; sometimes
you'd threaten to send me
to reform school. "Shut up!"
I'd shout from my battered mind
and run off from the bristling
battles to hide in the woods
and bathe in the frog pond to
make believe I was lying
in a coffin. When you found
me, you'd haul me
to Vacation Bible School.

And now in mid-life after
you've left us from Parkinson's,
I regret that I didn't ask
about your history
so I could be part of that spirit
ever attempting to understand.
Now I'd like to know what force
pulls me into that spare room
to catch a glimpse of you; then
to stare at your picture, with
steel-rimmed glasses over
hazel-blue eyes, light skin,
and your unsmiling, austere look.

For a Friend in Travail

> "A woman who tells the truth creates
> the possibility for more truth around her."
> — Adrienne Rich, *Women and Honor*

After your mother's death, and the children's
departure, mind dulled, hallucinating
on wine and Prozac,
you inhabited another.
We could not imagine your vision.
Stretch halfway round the globe and be part of it:
Sleepless after midnight. Clothed in a nightgown,
the flask on the way to Vermont,
through fragmented woodlands.

Specialist of artistry and independence,
what's happening to you now?
Crabwalking over the ledge, grasping
branches with forward-facing eyes, I imagine
that you will hang on there in the urban jungle.
Soon, in the remote mountains, we'll bathe
in hot volcanic springs and feel the falls
massage our shoulders.
How the Drinking Gourd empties itself,
we cannot say.

On the Beach at Crest Haven

Ten years ago, at Crest Haven, you reminded
me that I hid your coat when we were young
as we planted pansies and nasturtiums and set
a trap for field mice squatting in the shed.
You were weakened by chemotherapy then,
trying to recover from lung cancer.

At seventeen, I left home not to return until
thirty-five years later. You'd moved away
to New York and then to Sweden.
Our personas, I imagine as a moving tide
of cathartic and symbiotic gains and losses.

Now we're beachcombing on York Beach
in Maine. The weather's hot, that childhood
slight you still remember, but I want to deny it.
You didn't tell me then that it affected you so.
It restrains you; I now imagine I'm almost forgiven.
Hearing a frantic
cry, we look over and see an injured sea tern,
one leg caught by a marsh hawk on the sand.
I distract the hawk with my towel; the tern
stumbles with one leg wounded, tries to escape.
We kneel down; the tern stumbles with its injured
leg, escapes from the hawk, lifts its good leg,
attempts to raise its wings, eyes me with
a bloody look. While we chat, laugh, and forgive,
it hops on both legs, stumbling; flies.

Ode for the Family Reunion

One October morning, from fifty states,
family's roots nourished first in Plymouth Rock
trusting the clan's friendship,
they met in congress.

Granted a petition from the Meeting House
as belfry bells chime, auspicious
spirits flew in and out of wide-spreading trees.
Here they mustered amid cedar saplings.

Nine acres of oak-hickory-pine woods.
Some fallen pines where settlers
once planted their gardens, built cabins,
and mended fences
pasturing Guernseys and Holsteins.

The drummer called to arms. We listened to genealogy
levitating from Ye Olde Burial Grounds.
Historian souls searched the sanctum
as members promised repair of cemetery stones
grown old with lichens.

Descendents of families moved westward;
Mormons became the chosen government.
The land they enriched with strength.
Not running for reelection, "I'll prepare
a place for you," Governor Leavitt wrote.

The flags we raised in honor. I remember my forbears
and loved ones put into horse cart; placed in the ground
and my throat burned, like a sunburn over chemotherapy.
Pulling our divining rods,
some relatives want to come back

Arriving at Another Place

"Our attachment to the land was our attachment to each other."
—Terry Tempest Williams, *Refuge*

Some fifty years ago, my older sister and I tramped home
    from school, holding our arms open for our little sister.
Today, leaning on a crutch,
    my younger sister manages to hobble out of the group home,
        eyes bloodshot, arms self-mutilated.
All winter she has been waiting for me
    to take her out to the Ice Cream Shop
        for glazed donuts and strawberry sundaes.
She wants to taste the moment as another
    chocolate candy bar.

We arrive at the old homestead
    where she once gathered lilies of the valley
        by our two-room grammar school.
Some vision in my mind
    of father, mother and young sister stirring
        in buried grounds calls me.

I found our childhood farmhouse on Flag Hill
    with barn roof caved in next to overgrown orchard.
Nearby, the family's cemetery harbors phantoms
    drifting in a white pine grove
        by glacial erratics, bloodroot and purple trillium.
        Native ghosts and fading sunset
          unnerve me.

What keeps her waiting in the car unwilling to get out?
    I ask her, 'Why do you always
        stay inside and not walk around with me?"
But she pleads, "A prosecutor has marked me
    for extermination. Take the orders
        off me!" she cries.

"Remember how I used to take care of you?"
    I kneel, pressing plants down beside the graves....

11

Carol Leavitt Altieri

Ambushed

(For My Sister)

If solitude or fear, or pain, or grief, / should be they portion, with
what healing thoughts / Of tender joy wilt thou remember me, / and
these my exhortations!..../ That on the banks of this delightful
stream / We stood together; and that I, so long / A worshipper of
Nature, hither came....
—William Wordsworth, *Tintern Abbey*

From the stereo, Credence Clearwater
Revival singing: "I see the bad moon
rising. I see troubles on the way!"
And family and friends weave together

watching and praying. Cisplaten gurgles
in a glass bottle. Constellation
Scorpious rises on the horizon
like a lamprey eel leaving a bloody circle.

Then the silence like self delusion
by which I hope. And by which I struggle
to hold on. I hold, hug you and warm your
hands, "I'm not going to die," you whisper.
I imagine, how much you loved New England's
rural acres and camped in the White Mountains
at tree line.
We'll keep your treed lot in North Conway
to listen to the great gray owls at night time.

Elegy for Beverly

Many lives are moved from their warm haven
by my younger sister Bev's untimely death.

An original with triangular scar on her face,
skin freckled, eyes sapphire, hair tawny-blond;
now her muscular legs and curves displaced
blending with Stafford County's country land.

She sheltered friends, worshipped earth, nourished
us for forty-odd years, rocked and cradled;
wove stories, kept the family history's course,
hayed, planted, harvested and baked bread.

Her three grown children revere the earth
as she once did and did not hesitate
to plant a garden and stoke the hearth;
carry new-born calves home in a bloody state.

By the willow, a yellow-breasted chat nests
in flurry of goldenrod and Queen Anne's lace,
with black stripes on a chestnut-olive breast
and a triangle of black on a yellow face.

She drank from the spring of Acadia's roots
in Maine, after visiting Nova Scotia
where she, sister and mother were born
eating only dulse on the boat coming over.

Now I'm caught in a silken reverie
seeing her weave tapestries on a loom;
viewing her photographs of old-growth trees
while hearing her play harmonica tunes.

Her ex tried to play her like a jointed doll
but his acts needed many players, often;
he pulled his own strings in another dwelling
which drove her faster to her coffin.

Frogs gulped from the flowing Isinglass
River where after haying they were bound.
Joe-Pye Weed smothered the Purple Glasswort
and pine cones and acorns fell to the ground.

An Acorn Whistle for Bethany Wanderers

"Miranda: 0 wonder! How many goodly creatures are there here?
How beauteous mankind is. 0 brave new world that has such
people in't!"

The Tempest, Act 5

No high-tech razzmatazz here...
No laser beams shining on Elysian fields.
Only Bethany Wanderers with
muted halos stepping along in tribal order
on the Norfolk Trail.
following Barrie and Steve whose gifted
fingers like Rumpelstiltskin's make gold
from straw.

Viewing the trees as a flying carpet of color,
we rise above the hill to Roosevelt's hunting
lodge, witnessing chestnut and elm,
butternut and hemlock, attacked by monsters
of cankers and blight, yet still quivering
to redeem life.
Where migrating birds embroider
the sky, lakes and trees, Steve makes
an acorn whistle for us
and points his sacred wand touching
"Fairy Rings," then 'Witches Hobble,"
and "Dwarf's Fungi," showing us
how Lactarius threads the world together.

Then with winged mane, the flight
of Pegasus, in the forest
where genies from a spineless kingdom
rule the earth.

Visit With My Grandson

Near swaying sugar maples, you find
a painted box turtle with green frogs
jumping out of our shady backyard
pond. Away from the treadmill,
you pull my hand. The painted turtle
burrows as you wheel barrow
on Grandfather's
woodland gardens.

Some green frogs from Celebrated
Croakers' College close eyes to make
a leap of faith
as they catapult to stardom.
One, like a Calaveras' County
frog, kicks and springs into the air
—echoing Flag Hill Pond
on my childhood farm,
at the pasture's edge forty-five years ago,
in Andover, New Hampshire
under blue gaze
of Kearsarge Mountain.

We stand at pond's edge
bending our heads like turtles.
You free your hand
to touch one stretching his neck
to hear star frogs' songs.

Here links confide commentary.
My grandson and I marvel
at woodland creatures;
woods rich with mountain laurel,
swamp lilies, painted turtles, thrushes
and piping frogs.

Our measure of change
and reverence
and prayer.

The Loons Call

Even now, from afar, loons
call. I listen and weave
up Killington Mountain toward
the whistle cry. A ruffed
grouse shuffles through leaves
and ferns. In single file,
we follow a leader
like a religious order
of bowed heads.

Under a pagoda of spruce,
I clamber to the ridge outcrop
watching my footsteps—
on writhing roots that trip
the unwary.

Looking over the rim of the ledge, I see
the bonfire of bud-shaped peaks. Calm
breezes blend with our voices.
Feeling the family links
connect, I'm wary of rootless
moss growing on rocks.

We rest awhile near the mountain's
lake, the mist reflecting images
of thoughts unsaid and hurts
unhealed. From afar,
the loons call.

Over the granite boulders, I reach
for handholds embedded in soil,
down steep rock spines that overhang.
Crabwalking over ledges,
I push free reaching into
the pulse of the sky.

Divorce Trial

I stand in court
    for my last born, now a man,
once possessed by passion
    ten years ago; not knowing
how torn apart I was
    at the wedding ceremony
as both of us separated
    from our senses and I divorced
my soul's eye.

A phalanx of attendants
    in dark-feathered garb stride
to their places
    as a flock of starlings in backyard
sanctuary jostle at the feeder.

I hear a shrill call
    to arouse murrelet chicks.
I hear a call
    resounding the sunset.
I see a shrike hanging its victim
    on a thorny tree.
I see a blue heron driving
    its spear-like bill
straight to the mark.

Like the enduring bittern,
    what do I ruminate on now?
My eyes roll past
    all the faces in my head.
The soul drops down,
    yet the heart persists
        with mysterious desires.

The Marginal Way, Ogunquit, Maine

Mid-morning fog lifts. My daughter and I
    bound together from different spheres,
        feel pull of moon on ocean's tide

on rocky outcrops heaving out of coastal
    cliffs where glaciers gouged retreat.
        We pause on pathway, sit on the bench

as my sister and I once did
    sharing Coleridge's,
        "The Rime of the Ancient Mariner."

Today dwellings slope to hidden beaches,
    and children explore tidal pools of slate-blue
        mussels and rosy crabs in flotillas

of seaweed. Wary of slick-covered
    downward slanting-boulders,
        a giant snail's trail, we view

the ocean's glow of cobalt blue
    writhing away to the horizon. My daughter's hair
        glistens with sunlight like my sister Beverly's

forty-five years ago. I breath the essence of wild roses
    and beach plums covering rocks.
        Crashing surf in high swells

sounds against domes of granite and schist.
    Hymns emerge from shrubbery
        as swallow-tailed piping plovers wearing

black stripes on shoulders and brow
   come soaring in on ocean tides
      whistling their lonely notes.

Greater yellowlegs flutter in circles and huddle on rocky cliffs,
   feathered wings clutching mates and chicks;
      seeking green sea urchins that puff up spines

like porcupines. They anchor themselves to rocks
   in ocean water, clear as quartz crystal
      in tidal pools, most potent amber.

Going Home to Flag Hill After Forty Years

I returned to our ancestral
farm, baited my memory and drew in
the catch. Frog Hill Pond where we fished
still there along the twisting dirt road.

Across the road, where we pumped water
for long departed Holsteins and Guernseys,
now part of vernal dwelling place
for salamanders, bull-frogs and newts.

I delved into hollyhock garden savoring
the nectar. They are growing marijuana
in our pasture, where dad shouldered
me and stopped the bleeding when
the mad terrier tore my flesh.

Since then, I've journeyed far
from our unpaved road and orchard
to nectar my genetic pool
and probe meaning from Rosetta Stones
in the Cathedral of the Pines.

I've Been Traveling On That Interstate Highway

With fellow commuters
following the Siren Song of the city,
I wear charms and amulets around my neck
and secure a horseshoe on my seat.

We are drawn together
facing quadruple headlights
as incandescent light spills down
on the early morning throughway
in adagio rhythm like camel trekking
in Australia's outback.

Sandblasting gears,
monstrous trucks, road trains, gasoline drums,
orange-highway trucks, bulldozers, cranes,
car trailers, trailer trucks, 18 wheelers,
shift like giant boulders on deserts of sand.

Off by the side of 1-95,
a wisteria vine holds a spruce tree hostage,
and staghorn sumac turns brown.

Demons of road warriors
weave in and out of triple lines.
Like road suckers, they
overtake, wipe out
bear down and hold others hostage.
Manacled; Shanghaied!

Cars roll into ditches.
Trains jackknife as police in multi-colored cars
flash strobe lights.
Lanterns lure vessels onto coastal rocks.

With my little foot, I extend my body
pull back, undulate, and expand a half-mile,
retract a mile, and uncoil around obstacles.

Blanco Turbi and the Threatened Turtles

Blanco,
midwife of their mission,
stands waist-deep in the water
in faded blue cut-offs
bringing sea grass and jelly fish
so they won't be stranded
or taken for turtle soup
or tortoise shell jewelry
or even aphrodisiacs.

Flapping flippers like ocean wings
from the raging tide,
laden with crates of eggs,
the Armada struggles up the beach
beating at the heart of their existence
nose-to-ground returning
to cradle of their birth.

Blanco
patrols,
driving away
the squatters,
the poachers,
and the vultures.

Up the beach,
they drag their bodies,
digging, scritch, scritch, scritch
scratch, scratch, scratch,
with only their flippers
churning and slithering,
scooping out sand in
nest shaped like a watermelon,
dropping one egg at a time
and covering them
with flippers churning.

Blanco:
a Celtic dragon slayer
scattering all competitors
guides them back
to the ocean
past a gauntlet
of predators
full-throttle
before
the sun sets.

Cancun, Mexico

Hot sun suckles sap,
leaches the soil of nutrients
returns exotic flowers.
Limestone-shaped fossil sand
stays cool in sun.
Wind blows palm fronds
like a Mayan dressed in jaguar
skins thundering through thorn forest.
The feathers of his head dress
flutter in Gulf Stream wind.

Wind spirals itself into conch shells
whistles like flutes.
Palm fronds breathe coconuts.
Velvet purple Wandering Jew
is air-layered to bleached sand.
Wind plays with rainbow sailboats
as sailors struggle....
A rider parasurfs toward the sky
under a multi-colored parachute.

Iguanas in Cancun, Mexico

Green lace-patterned,
two of them
sunbathe on lichen-flecked rock.
You throw them a morsel of bread
and watch them flick
reddish-bladed tongues.
They leave a tiny
trail of sand riffling
with vestiges of
five-fingered hands.

Sawtooth-raised ridges,
plates of armor erect in motion;
with streamlined bodies
and whip-like tails,
they stare goggle-eyed,
freezing as if taxidermized,
except for pulsating throats,
as they
scuttle down
to rocky cave.
Descendents
of fearsome dinosaurs
we can hold them in our arms
for a quarter.

Summerland's Sanctuary

The Fairy penguins are smallest of 17 species; the only species to breed on the Australian continent. The Penguin Parade takes place every night of the year as ancestors have done for 1000's of years. 5000 visitors sit on tiered benches waiting to see them. In the dark the "huk, huk, huk" is heard as they magically appear at the ocean's edge and make their way up the beach.

Floodlights play on dark ocean
like an Easter Passion Play
around Phillip's Island, Australia.

We bound up the beach,
by tussock covered dunes
among pilgrims and disciples
to witness Little Penguin Procession.
In uncertain anticipation,
"Will they come tonight?"
The waves roll in and rush
back scrolling testimony.
A gaggle of little penguins submerge
and sweep out; scramble ashore
toddle across the beach corridor
like nattily- dressed feathered
monks in a holy day procession.

Little blue-black chatterers
with shearwaters and silver gulls
celebrating among congregations
sharing cave-like pews and altars.
Mates greet each other with gestures,
braying in antiphony, mewing
screaming, trumpeting, barking,
yapping, growling with chicks.

Public ceremony
of nature's *tour de force;*
moonlight scintillates
on dark ocean's scroll
while danger lurks underwater....
Human multitudes
clutching their prayer books
file off bleachers, trying
not to intrude.

No Chemotherapy for Dolphins

A dolphin caught
like a yacht on a reef,
a one-legged animal
staggering out of a trap,
flees invisible enemies.

Near bat caves, beach combing
Prince William Sound in June,
I step over barnacled
rocks and reddish-brown algae.
Summer breeze sounds
through broken glass.
"Every day, a new dolphin count."

Pale, skin stained red
and festering, yet lungs
still pulse
Sea lice disappear
into cave-like holes.

I hear a loon
sobbing a call, mad
with terror. Some serpents
shoot poisoned ink,
like out of the Apocalypse.
My prayers rise heavenward,
but there is no
chemotherapy for dolphins.

Exxon Valdez

Whirlwind sucks us
down, dumbfounded,
churning up purple algae
and blackened sand.

On the rainbow coast
near water's edge
in southern San-Francisco
a sea otter floats.

Blue fish
and pink crab legs
on bibbish chest,
tail oaring.
With flippers
a hovering mother
decrumbs his chest
piques his cheeks
and flips him over
on blubberous belly.

Much later....
sea mammals push north
to breeding grounds,
Valdez oil nets and traps
choking them
like Portuguese-man-of-war
jellyfish.

Plovers, Dowitchers and Sandpipers at Food Court Mall

In my young mind, it had something to do with the magic of birds,
how they bridge cultures and continents with their wings, how they
mediate between heaven and earth....It is a fertile community where
the hope of each day rides on the backs of migrating birds.
                            —Terry Tempest Williams, *Refuge*

Down to golden tan coast, a swoosh of wings
in synchronized flight, black-bellied plovers;
tawny dowitchers land next, stand out
in the crowd; then the sandpipers touch down.
All swallow to satiate, flapping their wings.

From the menu:
Midges, Crustaceans, Mollusks,
Beach Worms, Insects, Dragonflies, Beetles
Grasshoppers, Boatmen, Tiny Frogs
Seaweed, Small Snail Sandwiches
Plant Seeds and Fish Soup.

Honks and barks; glissando-arpeggios
rising again in synchrony, they catch a thermal
as wings reflect the sun.
Humans encroach on avians' realm,
taking their homes for mammon.

Carol Leavitt Altieri

Leased Lodgings of the Cliff Breeders in Iceland

From a myriad of flights
crisscrossing broad oceans:
an irrepressible force
overcome by mating desire,
in stacks like a stern-trawler,
on rugged cliffs of Westman Islands.

In the vast pantheon, the highest tier
the puffins, dressed with blue,
vermilion, white and green splashes,
dig long burrows in the cliff ledge.
Strutting about with fish catch, they
speculate on higher position in life.

Above the kittiwakes,
the guillemots of the auk family
dressed up with spectacles,
straddle conquered ground
swaying on small ledges
sometimes caring,
for neighbors' children.

In the middle tier, halfway up
the cliff face, unlike other colony
dwellers, kittiwakes construct
nests cemented to promontories,
brooding and keeping to themselves.

Below on next tier, the fulmars
stocky and stout, prefer
a two-story apartment
among sea grass and lichen ledges.
Parents shuffle on their tarsi
greedy for liver-fat and blubber.
They spit oil out at all intruders.

Near the base, the razorbills
with black backs and white bottoms,
choose broader crevices
among boulders of wet-sea plants.
Lying on their bellies parents urge
chicks to leap over the scree into the sea.

Shades of Altamira in Spain
recalling both early man
and these seabirds as cave dwellers.

Millennium Grove, R. I. P.

The first trees I got to know ... highly skilled veterans seasoned
in survival techniques. They had started fortuitously as seedlings....
They had shouldered past their siblings and finally pushed above
the forest canopy into the free blue sky where swallows wheeled
in summer and snowflakes whirled in winter.
—Ann La Bastille, Woodswoman

Giant sequoias, Temples of Time,
I offer you fragrant frankincense,
for thousands of years of growth
in your forests
of cedar, Douglas fir, sitka spruce,
and ponderosa pine.

Ferns genuflect under forest columns
under canopy like priests swinging
braziers of burning myrrh.
You were seedlings, saplings and shoots
when Neolithics lugged giant
stones for Stonehenge.

Groves of your ancestors sheltered
nomadic wanderers;
now a crown of branches cradle
a pair of rare murrelets
sending out whistling
cadences to the heavens.
You hold spotted owls,
offer shelter to salamanders,
and save spawning salmon.
Then your limbs are lopped off
and song sparrows are bloodied,
silenced in their nest.
A revving of chainsaws storms
your temples as trees plunge
and smash forest-loving creatures.

Earth movers come; chain your stripped
arms, pull trunks up by roots,
drive from the scriptorium;
and you're scavenged
to a chip mill that grinds your temples
up for pulp.

Spare the Elders

A crown of leafy branches
cradles a pair of marbled
murrelets sending out a whistling
cadence to the heavens.

Then the slash-and-burn ones
come with chainsaw gangs
and gold miners
bringing harvesters and skidders
to the largest stands,
sequoias and redwoods
alive for over a millennium.
All day until the setting sun,
sixty-foot band saws
with blades and skidders
pull trees to loader,
the fellerbuncher
like a huge scissors strips
trees in two giant bites;
grabs the hard, the soft,
the saplings, the living and the dead.

The earth splits and shakes
under root fibers.
Broken spiders dangle
beside chipmunk babies ripped out of nests.
And the black-throated blue warblers
in their moss-hair nest
with newly hatched eggs
are crushed on their first quest.
Skidders and bunchers revving,
cracking, roaring down the runway;
earthmovers stripping soil,
suffocating gills of salmon,
clogging streambeds of frogs.
Chipping and pulping,
leaving a gray stubble of humps.
What's left after Solomon's seal, wild ginger,
blood root are crushed,
Douglas firs, ponderosa
saplings, pine sprouts ripped
from the soil?

A butchered landscape
with piles of burned slash;
an automatic rifle rest
beside a battered tree stump,
against a misty-gray horizon.

One Step Ahead of the Hunters:
The Yanomamis Speak

The sun burns red through a shroud
as we wring the rain-chant ritual
and beat out the evil spirits.
A child's voice keens
in a grass-covered hut,
like a rivulet's last riffle.
We stare at the flames,
reflecting our homes
watching our huge ocean,
smoldering from our huts,
where we have prayed
to be faithful to the end.

For our blood-shot eyes
foam billows out of the river,
we can't lie down tonight;
or even sink into hammocks.

The planet's pulse
shallows and weakens
from the realm of the gold-faced
monkeys and the scarlet macaws.
Staggering through the smoke,
Antonio, our priest, promises
rain tomorrow.
But the next day, waiting for rain
we mistakenly take a drink
where hunters laid
out the poison bait.

We search in vain
for our comrades, seeking
the red howler monkeys
circuiting out on lianas,
from the skeletons of giants.

The passion flowers' soil
slides into the river,
and we draw on the ground
with the fearsome jaguar
looming in the savanna.

But as dawn breaks tomorrow,
the rain shower will pour
through the parched forest—
when we have beaten out
the hunters who stalk
like huge walking sticks
brandishing torches.

Memoir: Searching for Rare Bachman's Warbler

After hearing rumors that one had won
on playing fields of Darwinian survival,
I trek out to a small tributary,
giant stepping over holes
of Great Dismal Swamp,
slipping through grasping briars,
skulking in blades of marsh thickets,
defying ticks and green flies.

I brush aside feathered phragmites
swaying metronomic. Dusk nears,
as overhead in live oak canopies,
waylaid painted and indigo buntings
eavesdrop across the spires.
I cross woodland streams, scrambling
through sedges hearing serenades
of reed warblers shifting
ventriloquil songs in shadows.

My heart sinks; *there he is!*
The phantom from thick brambles,
the golden-winged, black-crowned warbler
with the sun's glint on his back
gamboling in beard moss.
A harpoon stab of connection
vanishes even as Audubon painted.
Am I chasing the last Bachman's Warbler
off the planet?

The Bachman's Warbler
probing deeper into blossoming orchids
lifts its rare voice
as candles flame in the wind,
striking a deeper chord of loss....
What music could console
after the last one?

Stuffed in a natural history museum
iridescent genes never to be restored
the DNA that might redeem us.

When I Witnessed the Blue-Footed Boobies

On Darwin's uplifted Galapagos,
under the golden canopy,
male and female blue-footed boobies
salute each other, high-stepping
and flaunting their blue-suede shoes
in a Lindy Hop; then a dude Jitterbug.
He, the King of Swing in prom garb
pirouettes around her, angling
his bill upward. She sways her neck
around as he sends up a shrill whistle.

She utters a cooing reply, then
shakes, rattles, and rolls in air currents.
Together they make the rounds of nesting
grounds among the tortoises,
shake hands,
enchant their audience,
set the stage.

Remembering Rachel Carson, 1907-1964

You haunt my spirit, like Pelé
Hawaiian Goddess, renewer of land, my muse.
Yes, we'll save stranded turtles and set
spiders free who borrow our cabin.

From the first time, I read your words
roused from the ashes of those toxins;
you were weaving *ologies* together
as Darwin's Mosaic of Species,
and who could challenge your biology?

I homed in to hear the rhythm
of ocean in cone-shaped seashells;
to find spiral wisdom in silver conches;
to witness one small fluttering form
enlightened with your Minerva's touch.

Your books about the earth
are heavenly bodies set in motion.
Your eyes of night vision, the
Dome of Heaven lit up as Van Gogh's
"Starry Night."

You probed the unknown
as astronauts in space shuttle, Endeavor,
and like a monk in a scriptorium,
wrote your holy books in stained glass.

It's painful as the fate of extinct warblers,
the land we taxed with sprays.
Still, we'll keep the robins from toxins
and ride the crowned crane of your kingdom.

While yourself, crushed by cancer,
scalded like hell fire. It ran over you—
Who will renew the pesticide-laced land now?
Our only planet we could ever live on.

Song for the Wilderness Champion

Bob Marshall hoisted over ledges
of Congress, stirred up men
in chambers, and told tales
of those who clear-cut
and burned creatures out of homes.

At times he sang and beckoned me
to follow the ancient trail: *"I love
to go a wandering until the day I die...."*
and my boots cushioned needles and moss
among others who hiked the forest ways.
I know he knew his compass and his maps.

Hearing his voice with Teddy Roosevelt's,
I hummed along with him as he hiked
ahead with his tawny retriever,
who portaged his loads and pulled him
out when he fell into the raging river.

Still he raced up peaks and carved
the Manifesto tearing down walls,
saving acres of wilderness in rambles
from Alaska to Cadillac Mountain
forevermore.

When he died, not by the paws of
the grizzly bear who howled him up
a tall pine tree, but at thirty-nine
on the midnight train to New York,
lovers cried, and his soul rose
to heaven through tree boughs.

Celebrating Spring

After Keat's *"To Autumn"*

Oh! Spring season of mosaic fullness
when air plants hang from canopies of dappled sun,
monarch butterflies sidle up to dogwood's bliss.
Communities gather for town
meetings and farmers tap the sap of maple trees.
Underground, ants are streaming on their quests.
Brown bats carry babies at their breasts
and skunk cabbage shoulders its way for bees.
Migrants stir on silent wings when nights cease
searching for juice in caverns of cells.

For lo! The earth keeps fortunes in store;
then the male bluebird applauds the female's find,
when a newt scrambles over earth's floor.
Look! Hummers suck sap after woodpeckers drill.
The preying mantis packs its weaponry hook
near gardens of ferns and fungi populations.
Mating, two puffins click together their thick bills,
and alewives and rainbow smelt forage in brooks.
Earth opens like cocoons giving bloom. Just look!
Then naturalists struggle to protect congregations.

Here are the songs of spring, natures' rhythmic way.
Hear *Mozart's Magic Flute* and *The Musical Joke* too,
imitating starlings, stopping the time of day;
and evergreens flame a feathery hue.
The wail of the loon floats over the lake, real forlorn!
Then the foraging fiddler crab holds its claw aloft.
Yet lo! Too many song birds disappear. Birders sigh.
Frogs bellow for a home for life unborn.
The trumpet vine grows wild to the cloft,
while a wave of warblers vanish in the sky.

Smith College Botanical Garden

At Smith, I studied the gardener's fruitful
landscape, enriched by a plant researcher
from Madagascar. Ancient trees of blissful
sap, extinct dawn redwood seeds from earlier
botanist's labor. Ash, spruce, chestnuts here,
with frog pond lilies next to an avenue.
You can take a Magellan venture clear
around the catalpas for a fragrant view.
Blue butterflies pollinate columbine
plants. Scope protean shapes of pollywogs,
watch tanagers flit in capes of eglantine;
hear avian songs in wetlands and bogs.

A rare wood thrush whistles in harmony,
protected on this migrant's lone flyway.

Your Symbol Is a Garden

Today a goldfinch found
your thistle seed as you
made a plot of land
a sacred place. Back
and forth carrying
field stones, your
footsteps latticing
acres of ground.

You sculpt brown-black
earth sending out
rhizomes, redeeming
soil with compost,
laying out seedlings
for future harvests.

Gardener of nightshade
and gatherer of apple-
blossom fecundity, you
grafted shoots of the New
World onto rootstocks
of the Old, finding your
source in a Jack-in-the
Pulpit flower.

In Beijing, There Are No Dawn Redwoods*

This poem begins with my strong emotional response to
Metasequoia or dawn redwood and then visiting Beijing China and
seeing no trees there. A dawn redwood tree was thought to be
extinct until discovered in a mountain hamlet in China in 1941. At
this time it was only known as a fossil tree. A Japanese botanist
introduced a new fossil species into plant taxonomy. Thus, a fossil
plant confronted botanists and others in flesh and blood.

On the third day
of creation, a fruit-bearing
tree sprouted.

Moses wrote: Noah
built his ark
from a cypress tree
in 5000 BC;
and twenty years ago,
I planted a dawn redwood tree.

It rooted and rose slowly,
like a medieval castle:
maroon-striated bark
under green miniature
fronds high as the Egyptian
obelisk in Regent's Park.

It shades the bloodroot
and jack-in-the-pulpit choirs
mixing cedar with cinnamon,
aroma of wild ginger.
With dandelion puffs
and a bright moon,
its lacey needles light
the way for brooding
warblers flying home.
Its roots, like my wrinkled
hands, clutch
and change the earth.

Its seeds, believed extinct,
were found in China.
Yet, it did not grow there
to protect from the tanks
of Tiananmen. In Beijing,
there are no dawn redwoods.

Carol Leavitt Altieri

Chimps in Camp Gombe, Tanzania

My blood quickens when I wriggle
like an iguana on the ground
hearing kiss-squawks and hoots,
through tangles of thorn brush
and spot some chimpanzees
kicking, leaping, twisting,
somersaulting, and playing tug-of-war.

Chimps swing around on forearms
swaying back and forth in a pirouette
free of earthly bonds,
unlike me in thick brush on my stomach.
I watch one mother
near me nestle her Buddha
body around her infant to suckle.
Her coat glistening; eyes moist
as we look deeply into each other's
pleading eyes as I remember
my first-born thirty years ago.

The next evening, I return to find
the mother chimp lying face down
unbreathing, her infant flinching,
holding onto her coat, silent
and afraid; not leaping, somersaulting
or pirouetting any more.

Night cicadas buzz in darkening
sky and the other chimps hide
in wilted trees.

Shelling the "Pearl of the Adriatic"

People emerge from basements
of rubble looking like grief
without tears. Near graveyard,
an old woman risks her life
to save her dog.

Now Dubrovnik faces the firing
squad. Serbian tanks bombard
land, sea, and mountain echoing
around city's walls. I wince
as they shell the old city,
spilling blood of humankind.

I watch the cross on the hillside
fortress set ablaze trapping Croatian
defenders. Sirens mingle with smoke.
Artillery explodes in ancient
monastery lit by flames.

Once I swam in the Adriatic
looking up at the fortress,
planted like a rare sea shell
on the blue ocean below.
In this Croatian city, I dined
on squid risotto
and drank the local wine,
mingling our voices
with Gypsy street musicians.

Later in the morning mist,
Dubrovnik is smashed like
a mortared Leningrad after
the siege, and peace confronts
an unwanted guest
across the corridors....

Carol Leavitt Altieri

The Human Scourge

We are Tutsis in Kigali,
we didn't kill anyone.
"You must return to your land,
we welcome you everyone."

"I must stay in Kibumba camp,"
moaned Gamba in ragged jacket.
"Although life is horrible here,
they will chop me with a hatchet."

I put on my coat to go out in the storm,
with others to go to Kigali.
Stoned to death by enemy soldiers,
we saw corpses in Pig Alley.

Thousands of them were orphaned
and hundreds separated from the tribe.
In the exodus from Rwanda,
we wish that we had died.

The Heavens Scourge Us Too

The refugees huddled in outdoor camps;
the rain came pelting down,
soaking the thatch of clumsy huts
slanted on a stagnant mound.

A shriveled Goma woman bent
her back towards the storm,
beneath a broken parasol
in Zaire that August morn.

A boy wept on the muddy earth,
deep wounded in his shoulder;
"Oh, kill me now, oh kill me now,
I'm scared of growing older."

His stomach was convexly arched,
his feet were swollen, too;
trapped in the "safety of the church,"
he should have fled, like you.

Glowworm Grotto in New Zealand

Tempting us from our wandering
and heartslave thoughts,
we shiver in flat-bottom
boat of cave with
bats, beetles, lichens,
and fungi sponging off algae.

My thoughts rise heavenward
evoked by minister's sermon,
"Sinners in the Hands of an Angry
God" Jonathan Edwards proclaiming
"You hang by a slender thread!"

Is this where dead spirits reside,
this Sistine Chapel of Glowworm Stars?
From where did they come
to black, blue-green
sky of forest netherworld?

Looking up at Milky Way Stars,
straws hang down from nests
as human's condition, slender
sinuous threads of fishing lines.
Glowworms paralyze midges
with acid as my thoughts hit and run
like unruly bats.

Bird, Blossom, Branch and Tree

Wandering down a country path
seeing the small violets at your feet,
you wonder about the design of a butterfly;
think about the redstart and the locust
in the same family
with string beans and wisteria.

Touch the intricacy of a warbler's feather
winding through valley and mountain;
feel the willowy river breezes
and the sun canopy that warms you.

Or ponder about the age of pyramids
built when the sequoia was a sapling,
cathedral spires reaching skies,
shaping spiritual landscapes.
Muir's Trees of Life
house spirits and saints;
then vanishing forests shorn
for pulp. It takes a hundred years
to grow the heartwood.

Carol Leavitt Altieri

Out of Elm Street, New Haven

Your mother and father from Amalfi,
rising in the microcosm of American
mobility brought you here, cradled
in your grandmother's arms
like ascending the summit
on a gondola
in a breezy atmosphere.
You look down on the landscape
from the casement window
the clothesline strung out
near the magnolia tree
where the bird bath slaked
thirst of finches and sparrows.

From the upstairs, I could see
your mother hanging out white
laundry like decorating a
Zuppa Inglese. Then the relatives
visited for *antipasto*
and *cappuccino* with *zambucca.*

Much later, you waved good-bye
without the usual fanfare. Fault-line
cracks. One generation gave rise,
to another and the two-story house
once caressed, closed its arms;
abandoned without pity.
Intruders cracked the glass
and a lost pit bull cowered
by the barbecue fireplace.
Paint blistered that your uncle
once bent over like a jeweler
carving Italian cameos.

The old neighborhood lost
its pulse and neighbors moved away
like tourists to safer landscapes.
Still, one renter ventured forth to plant
an oak tree restoring the deceased elm
on Elm Street
attacked by the fungus.

Carol Leavitt Altieri

Bats Transform the Night

Under blue-black sky
adorned with Milky Way,
wave upon wave
of little brown bats
ascend red barn eaves,
as moon brightens them.
Swirling and looping,
spiraling and scrolling
between shadows
around tulip trees,
they orbit.
Their ultrasonic cries arouse
our sleeping retriever.

I remember
one September visiting
a famous cave in Texas
where a great nursery
of Mexican free-tailed bats
were hanging by their toes
deep in the cave
as we are in mid-life,
shaping life into waving bands
on a circular journey
resounding all connections.

A whirlpool of brown bats,
high-pitched clicking,
undulating wings
glides over backyard pond.

Hypnotically. I feel fluttering
above me, touching, dwarf-like
under sparking stars,
scuttling on black-magic way
like their cousins bestowing banquets
of flowers and fruit.

Gold Nuggets

Outdoors today in Indian summer,
kneeling down to plant my butterfly bush,
with the Northwest wind sweeping down
a congregation of songbirds, I hear a volume
of a high, clear whistle, the joyful,
full-throated echoing of infectious bubbling
from the tops of sycamore trees.
The singing and calling flows out from
ruby and golden-crowned kinglets.
Diminutive royalty joins
titmice, chickadees, nuthatches
and juncos tucking into seeds and insects
twitching at hibernating beetles.
All together, rapt in flute-like whistles.

In the conifers,
they flit in sudden motion, circling
under branches fluttering wings
twirling under crimson, russet,
and golden leaves.
Then tossing up and down
like shuttlecocks in hallowed sun light;
and I'm a little girl again in New Hampshire
woods seeking nests of warbling thrushes.
The ruby and golden-crowned kinglets
no bigger than child's hands,
still perpetually energetic as I am,
lift me upward on their flights
to new realms of ecstasy.

"The Hardship of the Blue Cloud"

The Westman Islands in Iceland lie over a crack in the earth's crust.
A new volcano erupted unexpectedly in 1973, on Heimay, the
Westman Island which is inhabited. The 5,300 islanders were evac-
uated overnight. Lava and ash buried 1/3 of the town. After the
eruption, most inhabitants soon returned to Heimay to rebuild their
way of life.

I

After the volcano Surtsey hissed for four years,
strange lights like blue jets, red sprites,
frozen trolls appeared in the upper sky.
Sleeping for many years, Vestmannaeyjar
was groaning like an injured cormorant.
I felt little shivers in my bones
and heard crackling shots. The ground
around me rumbled, rocked and shook.
We knew another Surtsey was coming,
having grown up knowing
about Grimsvotn, Katla, Hekla and Helgafell.

II

The eruption began in a hay meadow
near father's pastureland. Setting out waves
of reddish-orange flashes, lava illumined dense fog.
Billowing clouds of ash and pumice spread
for miles. Volcanic bombs tinkled
and crackled rampaging like forest fires.
The sea beamed at red-hot molten lava.
Uprooted twisted trees formed a graveyard
of small skeletons with crooked arms
reaching skyward. Beneath the lava:
our country, wild with creation.

III
From the crater Hekla, I heard strange voices:
high-pitched gasps, wheezes and groans.
Lava flows churned down the roads and valleys
burying houses in dunes of magma.
Bombardment of fragments, stones
and pumice blasted and scarred our church,
making holes where reddish-black clouds appeared.
Yet still at Kirkjubaer, the stone monument
to Pastor Thorsteinsson killed by the Turks' invasion
stands, now 400 feet higher against the sky.

IV
In American Army helmets, the Rescue Crew
gagged on sulfur even though cloths
covered mouths. Valiantly, they pumped
fire hoses of cold water at hissing lava.
Clutching suitcases and photo albums,
families ran to waiting boats where
my old neighbor, Dora Gudlaugsdottir
fled with patients and Einarsson's
grandfather stumbled and fell on the way
to the pier. Our sheep, chickens, cows
and horses were airlifted,
except for some cows shot by the farmer,
Karlsson. Our island, a geologic
ghost ship quickly abandoned
by its passengers.

V

Six months later, transcending lament and grief,
some Icelanders moved back home and shoveled
through lava and magma.
They pitched tents before finding buried homes
digging into the ash to bake brown bread.
Others divorced and did not return.
Sea cabbage, sea carrots and sea beets
grew on the magma cliffs.
The wind caught spider threads of silk,
lifted and carried them here;
and silky willow seeds colonized pumice stones.

VI

Our island floats on molten layers of a mantle
plume. Under the magma mountains
lie buried the Temple of the Old Gods
where we Icelanders allude to *"The Hardship
of the Blue Cloud."* Like Jules Verne, we have seen
the center of the red-hot Earth.

Shoreline Showdown

Stretching to the river, it's
the great abbey: Hammonasset—
landscape of green-gold marshland
and woodlands visited with warblers
that set you off
like a rainbow trance.

Selectmen, computing taxes, sell out
elderly citizens and x-y-z ers
bound to shell-shaped land
and a community full
of newly-awakened passion.

The real estate developers
show off Utopian renderings,
always getting what they want.
They tear the land's flesh
and siphon life blood,
turning their backs
on living community.

While they bring scams,
we join the legions of soul-crushed,
threatened creatures.

Outsiders, rich with starched shirts
and bottomless pockets,
even now plot to return.

Homage to Jacques-Yves Cousteau

Cousteau moved us out of blind alleys
away from rocky shallows
where marine species underlie
our kinship with the fur seals,
dolphins, and the sea lions.

Often keeping out nuclear sites,
he protected the spawning rights
of dolphins, turtles, and seals
who homed in impure seas.
Many times, he
rescued sea creatures from defeat.

He brought us to tide pools,
on rocky Atlantic shoals
and urged us to abate
hemorrhaged wounds of marine fate
and heal sores that bled in crimson blight.

He docked his research vessels:
the Argo, Jason and Miranda;
led us to the rocky beach,
the tidal flat, the coral reef,
where dolphins joined pair bonds
hearing the echo-depth sounds.

Oh, how high a price we owe!
Cousteau knows about strife,
inspiring us to save all life
for future humans to know-
believing the sea's golden age
will come after the toxic deluge.

Above and below sea level,
Cousteau rose from tangled mire
and moon-burst with sea life;
led us to see heaven on dark nights
and melodious rhythm of creation's lyre,
bringing oceans' vast essence to light.

Carol Leavitt Altieri

Sestina: To Our Ancient Sea Relatives

The wind whips the breakers of the sea
as I slip on my snorkel and mask
and dive down to kelp garden plants
where I slither around with dolphins.
Stingrays look askance at unknown creature
and I shiver when scorpion fish

puff up sharp spines. Even scorpion fish
are garbed in this cathedral of stained sea
glass. I commune with my cousin creatures
while a squid squirts ink at my mask.
Eyeing me furtively are dolphins
who swim around with branches of plankton.

A jellyfish pulsates from plankton
and is captured by scorpion fish
raising goose bumps under my wet suit as dolphins
toothed and slippery scramble by in our sea,
with upstrokes of flukes splashing my mask.
From lurking in weeds, sea squirt creatures

emerge. Still I'm not afraid of creatures
who whip home to eat slugs hiding in plants
of the sea forest, fogging my mask.
Swaying around, I submerge with clown fish
spiraling down to lower level of sea.
Yet, I'm not lonely with diving dolphins

keeping me company. The grasping dolphins
gobble pup fish when sea monster creature
with forked tongue sends acid through sea
blood and flicks his tongue in forest plants.
Hiding in crown-of-thorns, tidal sea stars
escape from meat-eating corals masked

as waving kelp plants; sea squirts mask
themselves too as kelp. Three dolphins
submerged with sea lions prey on starfish.
I'm corralled by other masked creatures
scrambling away as they devour plankton
and I synchronize with my cousins of the sea
masking my nature like corals among sea stars.

Gondola Lifts Us in New Zealand

I became intimately acquainted with every tree inside a 400-foot
radius. What at first seemed like a dense stand of random
temperate zone vegetation-maples, spruces, hemlocks, beeches,
birches, and pines-gradually introduced itself as an orderly
congregation of unique individuals.

—Ann La Bastille, *Woodswoman*

Above the lake, the gondola
lifts us as the waning sun
needles lacebark trees
and honeycombs ranges
of mountains. The mist
like mother-of- pearl
snow floats us
to Coronet Peak tower.
We ascend, windswept
and tipping sideways
as the beaver's dam
of Maori sculpture
carillons the land.

We rise heavenward,
close to Kauri tree temples
gods of the forest,
thousands of years old,
giving their first and last
testaments in seeds.

Here Kauri trees reach and
shore up the sky as a parson
bird dressed in white collar
swells out his song.

Grand Canyon du Verdon

We fill our water bottles
and shoulder our bindle bags.
Laced by lavender plants,
we drink in the scent of wild thyme.

Full of vanishing clouds,
English Ann offers no promise,
no ease, only Provincial essence
the ascent to the summit
of Point Sublime.

Moiré blue mountains ride skylines
as we rhapsodists and reluctants
trudge the path edging sheer cliffs,
Grand Canyon du Verdon. Above
the tree line, we spread our board
and savor the free flowing
sweet green liquor of the Monks.

Later, our boots step over nurse logs
on forest floors
cushioned with mosses.
Then sharply over steep ascents
and creased ledges through ferns
that reach out to form another layer.

I strain at wheel spokes
like a workhorse pulling a hayrack.
Rock pieces slip and chute down.
Pulling my last hurtle to the dome,
I'm full of the prism of Point Sublime.
Looking down on Verdon Gorge,
rhapsodists' voices blend soft winds.

Fairy Penguins at Phillip's Island, Australia

In 1770, Captain John Cook
mapping Australia's East Coast
found communes of fairy penguins
gathering ceremoniously.
Another platoon of penguins
wearing life-jackets,
looking like blue gnomes
scramble ashore bearing treats.

Visitors came by ferry
laden with blankets
pulsing sweet anticipation
under the moonlight
to see the parade
of nattily-dressed penguins
in dark-blue layered cloaks
raft out of the waves,
calling "koo-rooh-ah, koo-rooh-ah,
huk, huk, huk."

They form a colony
with short-tailed shearwaters
and silver gulls
like a living coral reef.

In Cook's day, mariners watched
waves roll in and rush back
as gaggle of fairy penguins
jockeying for position
consulted in little knots,
climbed uphill
to honeycomb of burrows.

Bound to land and sea
they check for danger lurking;
streak underwater,
paddle after fare for chicks
waiting among coves in tussocks.
With guttural growls
chicks bray in antiphony.
After Cook's day, other ships
shoaled on coral reefs witnessed
white-breasted fairy penguins
toddling in moonlit parade.
Ancient mariners implored,
"Let's boil them down for oil
and sell the rest
to the Royal History Museum!"

Carol Leavitt Altieri

Lake District's Dry Stone Walls

Under a heather sky as morning breaks,
we trek the dales and clamber up the fells
near tarns and keeps and old stone walls. Our boots
crunch bracken, ferns and moss, while sheep
with sidelong looks make way to let us pass.

Here stone age farmers, Celts and Norse
summoned spirits to layer slate stones,
crossing fields with Herdwick sheep, on high moors.
Listen! I think I hear the Knights whisper.

Like the sorcerers of Hadrian's Wall,
Stonehenge and the Pyramids, they quarried
rocks for dry-stone walls, clutching
stones of quartz and granite.
As before, I think I hear the knights whisper.

They tell us tales of those who built stone walls
high in the fells in wind and rain and sun;
who sculpted slate on stone mid fragrant fern,
forever praying to some ancient force
that was and is and shall be evermore.

On the Trail of the Sky Dancers

Skeins of sandhill cranes
wearing red top knots greet
some whooping cranes
in willowy plumes.
Once they guarded imperial thrones
of Beijing's Forbidden City
and pulled the chariot
of immortal souls of sages
going to heaven.

I scanned the sky
of the flock over the Oregon Trail.
They glided to a landing
braided from all compass points:
Platte River, Nebraska
along Great Plains
and Rio Grande
below Dragon Snow Mountain

In ritualized choreography,
a courtship display
shoehorning onto staging area
among cottonwoods and willows
spiraling; springing into the air.

Heads point heavenward
cranes watching the stars
trumpeting untamed nature.
Legions of them, some twittering,
most others dance, leap and whirl
spiraling upward in ascending flight,
flapping and spreading wings apart,
treading and remaining airborne;
tossing green streamers into the air.
Pan's lips playing pipes joining
the voices of poets, musicians and gods.

Carol Leavitt Altieri

The Endangered Roseate Terns of Faulkner Island

As if the island stones
had sprouted wings and fins,
roseate terns and relatives
grace the skies above us,
bearing alewives to mates and chicks.

Creating a thriving land home,
Father Spendelow
believing in the sacredness
of endangered creatures
shields roseate terns
from shrilling calls of warnings.

We once grieved roseates' passing
annihilated for fashionable
hats and battered
by wild marauders,
such aristocrats congregating,
now hold their ranks.

Our guardian ensures their survival,
making an oasis,
keeping watch over their domain
inviting terns to linger awhile
from epic journeys to mate
and transcend refuge places.

Roseates and relatives rise above;
wheel, swoop, and whirl over us
filling the air with clamoring,
"Zreep, Zreep, Zreep, Zreep!"
soaring on currents
working their aerial gyrations.

Terns glean our thoughts even
as they target our heads
mocking our limitations.

Like celestial forces,
roseate terns assemble
to stream scattering to the seven seas
searching for the vanished flock.
Reaching out to the unknown
as aurora borealis,
invisible forces commingle.

The View from My Backyard

I thought it was a demilitarized zone
as between North and South Korea,*
a haven for woodland birds: hermit thrushes,
rose-breasted grosbeaks
and black-throated blue warblers.

For all my life,
I thought it would remain,
lush woodland that sheltered
the emerald jewels of summer;
earth hues in autumn,
a playground for chipmunks, squirrels
and foxes.

Until one day....
I thought frost came dropping like death
browning everything in sight
nine whole acres—bare,
nothing left
except strangled tree roots.
All night, the bulldozer and crane
must have done their work in the darkness,
now reclining
with guards trumpeting warnings to trespassers.

The shagbark hickory where I gathered nuts
remains in my thoughts,
and the creek runs red with mud.

The homeless family of foxes in the darkness
prowled the neighborhood
breathing their last
before being struck on Route 1.
Dispossessed animals like phantoms
clandestine in shadows of condos.

*In 1953, North Korea was separated from South Korea by a zone of land
2.5 miles wide and 151 miles long. People can not go there. It is a peace-
ful place for cranes; a wildlife haven.

The Road to Sertang Temple

A monk speaks,
"The hidden land is finished."

I'm awakened as a flock of golden
plovers in winged poise scatter
like flying rainbow fish.
I seek the Gold Mandala
trekking in the Himalayas,
hiking to secret falls,
fern-bordered rocks,
paddling up rivers to beyul*
among ice peaks,
traversing mountains
inscribed with snow.

Water torrents cascade from cliffs
and wind hums among oak trees.
Our prayer flags tatter and tear
as we take the perilous paths
trudging over cliffs in smoky fog
capturing the soul of silence.
Juniper scents envelop hillsides.
Chortens* of Buddha engrave
stone walls by caves of saints.

A lama chants, dances, burns incense;
monks in royal-colored robes meditate.
In the courtyard, musk deer and wild goats
are sacrificed in the chasm
where hanuman langurs* once lapped
holy water.

79

Carol Leavitt Altieri

We cross the bridge where forest fires,
fanned by winds,
roar through gunmetal air.
Under clouds we camp in the meadow
with the vision of the Valley of Bliss
floating off into the galaxy.

beyul, remote sanctuaries
chortens, universal shrines symbolizing the one Buddha
hanuman langurs, a slender, long-tailed Hindi monkey of the genus
Presbytis.

Peterson's Poem

"I would like to believe she is reclusive at heart, in spite of the communal nesting of her species. I would like to wade along the edges with her, this great blue heron."
—Terry Tempest Williams, *Refuge*

We are trespassing in great
blue heron's territory,
only a foot away,
touching summer plumage,
ruffling feathers, feeling
nobility on the prowl.
Gulls sound, dipping
and swerving.

Not far from heronries,
darting spear-like
for fish and frogs,
great heron spreads wings,
bows, stretches, changes guard
in ritual feeding ceremony.

Together, sandpipers and I
taunt heron, sneaking up
while other self-serving
humans corkscrew in sand
running a different course;
dark cormorants fly over.

In Elegant Trogan Country

"Hope is the thing with feathers that perches in the soul."
—Emily Dickinson

We twitchers trample out
before the sun caresses
in Cave Creek, Chiricahua.
Trudging up canyon's spiral staircase,
where nocturnal toads tunnel
in the ocotillo, we search
for elegant trogans. Hiding
tenaciously, their suits
pack into oak cavities.

Snug sheltered inside
like old-fashioned hermits,
still elusive, male and female
sprint from shrubs to sycamore cavity.

The pair share in wealth
of sapsucker's lobotomy.
Male luminescent with
green-blue back plays his hand
"A Dealer's Choice."
He puffs out his rosy-colored
breast; then koinks his
"koa, koa, koa," strung-out call.

In vest and white ruff, flashing his
white tail fan-like, he tees up
in the sycamore.
Cat-eyed the couple sit upright, calling
"kow, kow, kow, kow,"
the prelude to our chase. Over and
over and over they call....

Like a game of poker,
Mother Nature bluffs and raises.
While here, she gives us
"A Grand Slam!"

Bushwhacking the Trail

Winding up ridges and down gorges
    from windy Camel's Hump
       to Smuggler's Notch,
my life's been carved by glaciers
    into domes and canyons; now
        a boreal forest over partridgeberry.

Warbling thrushes flit from blossoms
    to branches and woodland frogs
       along streams make our spirits
        dance like bacchantes.

Saw-whet owl pursues the weakened ones
    as I hear the whirr of merlin's wings
       making aerial dives for prey.

Sundew plant lures to trap door
        duping its victims.
Purple trillium, *blood root, columbine,*
   jack-in-the-pulpit color the trail
       as algae and fungi give and take.

White pines provide the pagoda tiers;
    all of life clamoring for position.

I listen for rare birds' call
    of ivory-billed woodpecker
       in bottomland forest.

My home, a Holy Grail;
    newts, frogs and chameleons
       gyre in Stratton Pond.

Across the marshland,
    a heron, silent watchtower
        immobile in shallow slough.

At the Ocean's Edge of Peggy's Cove

The sun silvers St. John's steeple.
Some gnarled pines left
where Micmacs wigwamed
and the soil swept away
into the vast silver-blue ocean.

Now a purple Pitcher Plant
bends its head seducing
a green fly like a lobster trap
and periwinkles shut their doors
as a Least Tern clutches a sand eel.
Limpets and barnacles stand up
to the pummeling surf.

In years past, when the run
was on for herring and mackerel,
the strong had squatter's rights.
Other creatures struggle today
near the ocean's edge.
Salmon hide by the shore
clutching smaller ones
with talons of eagle sunk
on the salmon's back.

Next year, the fishermen say,
the herring
will return. A cove of shifting views;
white washed the lighthouse stands.
Sandpipers in transit
from nesting rounds move on.
I see things not alone,
but connected and linked
to all other congregations.

Plovers turn in unison
as a host of shorebirds in fall plumage
fill up for the South American flight.
I wonder about their mystery
Each season, I ponder how they
make it, year after year and miss
the many who don't return.

Villanelle: Green Sea Turtle

(A lone sea turtle seeking to mate and nest.)

She traveled a thousand miles through open seas
ancient, unchanged from prehistoric swamps
gently imposing her nobility.

With all creatures from sea slugs to blue whales
she hunts Casseopia in currents of streams.
She wandered a thousand miles through open seas.

Her alliance of dependence on sea stars
working her passage through amber kelp realms
gently imposing her nobility.

Her kin: sisters, brothers carry wounds and scars.
Tattered barnacles use her for their sails.
She traveled a thousand miles through open seas.

Slaughter shadows over her carapace.
Along for the ride travel ocean snails
as she gently imposes her nobility.

Paddling with strokes of fore flippers racing
her home beach beckons but there is no male.
She traveled a thousand miles through open seas
gently imposing her nobility.

Carol Leavitt Altieri

Pilgrimage to View the
"Marsh Gods of Hokkaido," Japan

We danced in celebration
with ancient race of Ainu people
to see the surviving Japanese
red-crowned cranes,
"bird chariot of immortal sages."
During last century
they followed into oblivion,
ancient Ainus depletion.

In Kushiro marsh,
resounding triumphal calls,
a convocation of pairs, families,
yearlings and chicks,
rescued by farmers
warding off evil spirits.

In farmers' fields, dressed
in heavenly clothes of red crowns,
white plumes raised above their heads,
cranes glide through high-tension wires
in throaty-trumpeting voices.

Waving, flapping wings, leaping,
throwing tufts of grass like garlands
in prelude to courtship dance,
bonds strengthened
by synchronized postures.
Cranes worship shifting seasons
as brown frogs chime out in chorus.

Does the call of mysteries unveiled
make the flock so brave
in once wild and sacred place?

Amidst the meadow mist,
craning toward each other,
with a clear view of danger—
above white-tailed eagles,
below red-tailed foxes.
Sentinel cranes corral their flock
scampering wildly in chevron flight
as Ainus swirl and swoon
in plant-woven robes of earth colors.

Arrivata: Hawksbills

Hunted for tortoise shell by many nations,
turtle carapaces more highly prized
than ivory.
And take the time to come along with me
to Rancho Nuevo on the sandy berm;
we'll witness ancient nomads return
and herald the turtles' *arrivata*...
Fully-grown bodies roughed,
and heaved by flippers onto trucks
by market traders.

Marvel at their heads, marble-patterned,
buffeting waves as ocean surface roils.
Headstrong turtles follow mysterious impulse
when moon, tide, wind, weather
align.
Watch as they swipe flippers across their faces;
turtle tears washing away time and threat.
Scutes, mottled yellow, amber, brown,
rare flotilla coming home to the sand.

Wild Kingdom of Red Maple Wetlands

Beyond the noisy throughway
behind our Audubon Shop
a fragment of rich woodlands;
a brook flows under fallen leaves,
where developers see condominiums.

Here I seek solace with painted turtles,
salamanders and other wetland creatures
alive among shadows.
I raise my binoculars
to look at luminous maples
and blue heron nest as first-year herons
hungry for fish and frogs glide down
landing on fallen leaves along the stream.
Rufous-sided towhees
search and scratch warily
in undergrowth of cat's briar.

Above, Eastern kingbirds sweep
sunlit crowns chasing iridescent dragonflies.
The sun reminds me to leave but I stay
to watch for one last time
the burrowing of painted turtles
and non-Odysseus hatchlings.
Just then, a stream of thrushes
like flying flutists pass overhead.

Others will meet tonight
to change the wetlands' boundaries.
I stand here transported
from a scale of human terror
that all this life cannot comprehend.

Hiking by Silversword Loop

On the cinder lava landscape
nourished by scrunchy soil
on Sliding Sands Trail
of Haleakala,
a spiky-haired Silversword

stroked by Menehunes'
spiral wand
and nectared by orange
butterflies, flowers fragile
as Perseid meteors
streak white
across the sky.

They were taken to the Orient
for dried bouquets
uprooted by mountain goats
rolled like snowballs-
now like spun glass ornaments
after a fire.

Emerging slowly
from lava landscape,
a silk candle shimmering
in misty dusk. Viewing
Eden, I was just hiking by.

Quick Witted Entertainer

Our catbird
wearing black cap,
dark gray over light,
rusty brown undertail,
flicks about in bull briers,
loving the red mulberry.
Ventriloquist: mewing, croaking
clicking cricket arias
in a many-tongued comedy.

Nesting in shrubbery
he perches nearby,
laughs with me while
listening to his cousin,
the mockingbird sing in
hawthorn tree. He pauses,
sputters and hisses
the mocker's song.

Having the limelight
composer and improviser:
cackles, chuckles, connives.
My rollicking companion
singing for his dinner,
struts, impresario,
increasing the magic
of the avian world.

Carol Leavitt Altieri

The Wild Horses of Smoke Creek Desert

Roaming the high plains
the wild horses:
nostrils flare,
coats glisten, eyes moist,
manes flying,
they gallop one after another,
tawny, jeweled under the sun.

Wild horses roam grazing spaces
now herded by the helicopter
funneled
by Judas horse into fenced trap;
bottle-necked and jammed-
into oversized trailer.

The high plains' wild horses stampede,
flinching
on unknown way,
for adoption or the slaughterhouse.
I cannot forget their eyes, wild
with fear.

Sage brown in the sun
wild horses are captured.
All the creatures of the plains'
their stunning beauty
shake me into a gasping sadness,
powerless to intervene.

Prevailing

The beauty of woodland flowers is that they exist at all. Finding a
painted trillium or a pink lady's slipper elicits exclamations of admi-
ration, as much from surprise that such a delicate flower is thriving
unattended as from an appreciation of its form or color.

—Roger B. Swain
Earthly Pleasures: Tales From A Bioloqist's Garden

I found them at the edge
of the land
where it is still unpaved, unsmirched.

The crocuses,
in their necklaces of clover green,
bowing down to touch the earth,
their tips of petals
touched with emeralds.

Ahead of themselves, bulbs
packed away for another Spring
like some people always looking ahead,
stalwart even in a late snow.

Carol has completed graduate study and was awarded the Certificate of Advanced Study (C. A. S.) at Wesleyan University in 2001 after receiving a Masters Degree in English and a Sixth Year in Educational Leadership at Southern Connecticut State University. While there, she received "Graduate Poet of the Year." In 2003, she has been accepted into the Arts and Science Doctoral Program of Union College and University in Ohio.

As recipient of an English Speakers Union's Scholarship, Carol has studied English literature and culture at the University of London for two summers and participated in the Yale/New Haven Teachers Institute for six years. Also, she has won five Celebration of Excellence Awards from the New Haven Public Education Fund Presently, she is an English/Science teacher and Curriculum Developer in New Haven schools and teaches an environmental seminar and poetry workshop to high-school teachers.

She participated in three National Endowment for the Humanities Seminars: "Chinese Literature and Culture, Since 1900," "The War in the Pacific," and "Poetry and Plays of William Butler Yeats."

Aside from writing and teaching, she enjoys her grandchildren, cinema, hiking, birding, nature study, and reading: natural history, novels, poetry, and nonfiction.